GCSE
Science
FOUNDATION COURSEWORK
STUDENT'S GUIDE

Bob McDuell & Chris Sherry

Every effort has been made to trace copyright holders and to obtain their permission for the use of copyright material. The authors and publishers will gladly receive information enabling them to rectify any error or omission in subsequent editions.

First published 1998

Letts Education, Schools and College Division,
9–15 Aldine Street, London W12 8AW
Tel   0181 740 2270
Fax   0181 740 2280

Text © Bob McDuell and Chris Sherry

Editorial, design and production by Moondisks Ltd, Cambridge

All our rights reserved. No part of this publication may be reproduced, stored in a retrieval system, or transmitted, in any form or by any means, electronic, mechanical, photocopying, recording or otherwise, without prior permission of Letts Educational.

British Library Cataloguing-in-Publication Data
A CIP record for this book is available from the British Library

ISBN 1 84085 121 X

Printed and bound in Great Britain

Letts Educational is the trading name of BPP (Letts Educational) Ltd

Contents

Introduction   4

Getting started with Sc1   5

A close look at Sc1   6

1 Skill Area P   11
Planning experimental procedures

2 Skill Area O   17
Obtaining Evidence

3 Skill Area A   25
Analysing evidence and drawing conclusions

4 Skill Area E   31
Evaluating evidence

Your final mark   37

Introduction

This Letts Science Coursework Student's book has been specially designed to help you understand how Sc1 assessment works.

It is for students taking:

- GCSE Science Double Award at Foundation Level
- GCSE Science Single Award at Foundation Level
- Certificate of Achievement Science.

First write your name and teaching group on page 5.

Now read the **'A close look at Sc1'** section on pages 6 to 10.

This describes how the Science course is divided into Attainment Targets.

It also describes the four Skill Areas in which you are assessed and how your teacher will award marks.

The skills are very important parts of your examination.

We have missed out the very high level (grade A* to B) type of work.

We suggest that you work through the units in order.

Look at the examples carefully.

These will help you to get started and score higher marks.

Your teacher can help you to check your answers.

Use this booklet at the same time as you are doing practical work.

You can then build on what you know and can do as you finish each experiment.

Getting started with Sc1

A course booklet designed to help you get started with Sc1

For students taking

GCSE Science: Double Award   Foundation Tier

GCSE Science: Single Award   Foundation Tier

CoA Science

Name

Teaching group

A close look at Sc1

This table shows how marks are allocated to each Attainment Target.

	Attainment Target 1 -Sc1 (Investigation)	Attainment Target 2 -Sc2 (Biology)	Attainment Target 3 -Sc3 (Chemistry)	Attainment Target 4 -Sc4 (Physics)
Science: Double Award	25%	25%	25%	25%
Science: Single Award	25%	25%	25%	25%
Science: Certificate of Achievement	This depends on each examination group. At least 25% is allocated to Sc1.			

Sc1 is called **Experimental and Investigative Science.**

This Attainment Target gets you to use what you know about Science to show how you can investigate.

During years 10 and 11, your teacher will assess four **Skill Areas.**

These are called:

- **Skill Area P – Planning experimental procedures.** This is when you plan your experiment.
- **Skill Area O – Obtaining evidence.** This is when you do your experiments and write down the results
- **Skill Area A – Analysing evidence and drawing conclusions.** This is when you look at your results, plot graphs and write conclusions.

Skill Area E – Evaluating evidence. This is when you look at how well you have done the experiment. You look at how good your results are. You can also suggest how you could improve what you have done if you were able to do it again.

You will be assessed several times during your course.

Normally, only your **best mark** in each Skill Area counts towards your final mark.

If you are taking GCSE

In each of Skill Areas **P, O,** and **A** you can score up to **eight marks**.

In Skill Area **E** you can score up to **six marks**.

This means your maximum mark can be **30**.

This is then doubled to **60** marks and up to **three** marks added for your spelling, punctuation and grammar.

If you are taking CoA

Ask your teacher to explain what will happen to your marks.

When teachers mark work, they use a set of **criteria**.

The tables on pages 9 and 10 show you what you have to include in your investigation to get good marks.

They are written in a simpler language to help you to understand them.

Your teacher can award you marks in between what is shown in the table.

If your work is better than two marks for planning but not good enough for four marks, your teacher could mark the work as three.

Every time you do an investigation, use the boxes to tick (✓) what you have done.

This will help you to get the best marks you can.

Whole investigations

A whole investigation is an experiment where you plan the experiment, do it, record your results, analyse them and evaluate what you have done.

You get a mark for each of the Skill Areas.

Part investigations

You can plan an experiment which you never do. This is a part investigation.

Your teacher can give you a mark for skill P.

Your teacher can give you a plan. You can do the experiment, record results, analyse them and evaluate what you have done. This is another part investigation.

Your teacher can assess Skill Areas O, A and E but not P.

In all GCSE syllabuses, at least one mark has to come from a whole investigation.

A close look at Sc1

> Each column is for one investigation.
>
> Put a tick in the box every time you have been successful.

Planning experimental procedures

mark	When planning my investigation I have:	sugar					
2	planned a simple and safe experiment	✓					
	made sure that my experiment is fair						
	made a prediction						
4	chosen sensible apparatus and listed what I have used						
	used my scientific knowledge to plan my experiment						
	written down what things I am keeping the same						
	written down what things I am going to change						
	chosen at least five values for each thing I am changing						
6	used a wide range of values, not ones close together						

Obtaining evidence

mark	When doing my investigation I have:	sugar					
	used the equipment safely						
2	made some measurements						
	made enough relevant measurements						
4	recorded the measurements in a table of results						
	made at least five measurements for each variable						
	made all measurements as accurately as possible						
	repeated all of my readings and found an average						
	recorded all of my results in a table						
6	made sure that my table has headings with units						

Analysing evidence and drawing conclusions

mark	When analysing my investigation I have:	sugar					
2	written down, in general terms, what I have found out						
	drawn a graph or bar chart						
4	described the shape / trend of the graph or bar chart						
	labelled the axes of the graph with quantity and unit						
	drawn a line of best fit, maybe missing out some points						
	shown all my working, if I have done a calculation						
	made sure that my conclusion agrees with my results						
6	used scientific knowledge to describe my results						

Evaluating evidence

mark	When evaluating my investigation I have:	sugar					
	commented on whether or not I used the best method						
2	written a critical comment about the results I got						
	stated how accurately I was able to measure quantities						
	identified any result which looked out of place						
4	suggested how to improve my method						

We are going to look at each Skill Area separately and find out what you have to do to get good marks in each.

We will use a practical investigation to help us:

What affects how quickly sugar dissolves?

Skill Area P
Planning experimental procedures

There are some important points you must know before you start planning.

- When you are asked to plan an experiment, you should be able to use what you know of Biology, Chemistry and Physics to help you plan.

- When you plan, you should try to make a **prediction**.

  You do not have to make a prediction, but it is a good idea to do so if you can.

  Try to explain your prediction using your scientific knowledge. You can often find more information in your textbooks. Do not copy out whole sections but choose suitable parts.

- It is important to understand the term **variable**.

  A variable is anything that is measured or controlled.

  Most experiments will have a number of possible variables. The most important ones are called **key variables**. You should identify key variables and think about how to control them.

- Think about how many observations or measurements you are going to make.

- If you are going to plot a graph, it is usual to make at least five sets of measurements. These should be spread out over the full range of your experiment, not close together.

For example, if you are carrying out experiments between room temperature and 60 °C

20 °C, 32 °C, 41 °C, 48 °C, 59 °C would be better than
20 °C, 50 °C, 52 °C, 56 °C, 59 °C

You do not have to choose 20 °C, 30 °C, 40 °C, 50 °C and 60 °C

- Make a list of all the apparatus you are going to use.
- Write down any safety precautions you take.

Now let us look at the investigation 'What affects how quickly sugar dissolves?'

There are many variables we could choose to investigate.

Make a list of five things we could change.

1 _____

2 _____

3 _____

4 _____

5 _____

You probably wrote down things like:

type of sugar

amount of sugar

amount of liquid

stirring or not

temperature of liquid.

When you write **amount** you may mean **mass** or **volume**.

Try to be exact and state which of them you do mean.

If we decide that **mass of sugar** is going to be the thing we change, **time to dissolve** will be the thing we measure.

Our plan might read like this:

> I am going to add different masses of sugar to water and see how long each amount takes to dissolve.

We have planned a simple, safe experiment and the teacher might give us two marks.

We have put a tick in the two-mark box on page 9.

If we want to get more marks, we have to think about a **fair test, making a prediction** and **choosing the right apparatus**.

Fair testing means keeping all the other things the same. These include:

> starting with the same volume of water
> keeping the water at the same temperature
> having the water in the same type of beaker
> using the same type of sugar
> same amount of stirring.

If we just say that we will keep other things the same, we are showing the teacher that we understand about fair testing. We can put a tick in the fair test box on page 9.

We are on our way to scoring four marks.

Next we have to make a prediction.

What prediction can you make? Write it down.

_____

_____

_____

_____

Ask your teacher to check what you have written. If it is correct, you can tick the prediction box.

Next we have to choose our apparatus. Figure 1 shows some common pieces of apparatus. Write the correct name of each piece of apparatus in the table.

Choose your answers from this list.

beaker	gas jar	thermometer
filter funnel	test tube	evaporating basin
stop clock	clamp stand	
balance	measuring cylinder	

Put a tick next to the apparatus we should use in our investigation.

Figure 1

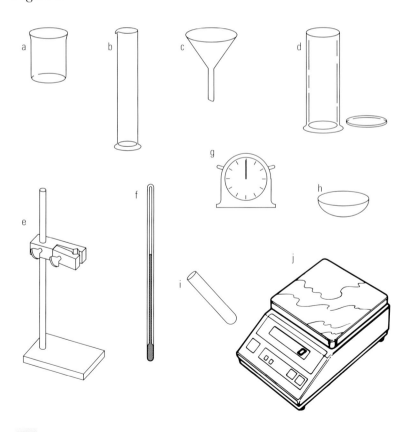

	Name of Apparatus	✓
a		
b		
c		
d		
e		
f		
g		
h		
i		
j		

You should have put ticks against **beaker, measuring cylinder, stop clock** and **balance**.

You may have put a tick against **thermometer** to check that the water is always at the same temperature.

If you have got the names of the apparatus right and just put ticks in the correct boxes then tick the apparatus box on page 9.

Four of these pieces of apparatus in Figure 1 are used for measuring. Finish the table.

Piece of Apparatus	Used to measure
	volume
	time
	temperature
	mass

We have now done enough for our teacher to consider giving us at least four marks.

We have already written down the variables we are keeping the same and the variables we are changing.

We must now choose different masses of sugar to use. Which set of masses of sugar would you choose to use?

A. 1 g   2 g   2.5 g   3 g   25 g
B. 5 g   10 g   15 g   20 g   25 g   Answer ☐
C. 25 g   50 g   75 g   100 g   125 g

A has five different masses over a good range, but the first four are very close together.

B has five different masses over a good range and equally spaced. This is the best answer.

C has five different masses over a very wide range which may be too large.

The only thing we have not done so far is to use our scientific knowledge to help us plan our experiment.

If we leave our planning at this point, our teacher may consider giving us five marks.

2 Skill Area O
Obtaining evidence

There are some important points you must know before you start making observations and measurements.

- If you do not know how to use a piece of apparatus, ask your teacher for help.

  You are going to be making measurements as accurately as you can.

- You must write down all of your observations or measurements.

  Do this as you make them. You will not remember them later!

- It is usual to make all measurements to the same number of decimal places.

- It is best if you record your results in a table.

  Design your table before you start.

- Look at the observations and measurements as you make them.

  You may see a result which looks out of place. Repeat it.

  It is a good idea to make all measurements at least twice and find the average.

  This improves the **reliability** of your results.

  If you don't repeat readings at the time, it may be too late.

Now let us think about our investigation.

We are timing how long it takes for sugar to dissolve.

We will be reading a stopclock or stopwatch. Most stopclocks and stopwatches used in schools have a digital display which looks like this.

$$00:00_{00}$$

The 00 before the : tells us the number of minutes.

The 00 after the : tells us the number of seconds and the smaller 00 the hundredths of seconds.

After one experiment, the stopwatch looks like this.

This means 1 minute, 24.73 seconds.

In our results table, it is best to use just seconds.

Since there are 60 seconds in one minute, we would write 84.73 s. This is 85 s to the nearest second.

Try the following examples. Change the stopwatch readings into seconds. Put your answers in the middle column.

	Time in seconds	Time to nearest second
$02:42_{55}$		
$06:02_{98}$		
$03:00_{01}$		

Ask your teacher to check your answers.

Do we have to measure the time to the nearest hundredth of a second or is that too accurate?

There are times when we can be too accurate and our investigation is one of them.

Next to your answers for the time in seconds, write down the time to the nearest whole second. Ask your teacher to check these answers.

We could have decided to change the temperature of the water instead of the mass of sugar.

We can usually read a thermometer to the nearest $\frac{1}{2}$ °C.

What are the readings on these thermometers? Write down the temperatures in the boxes.

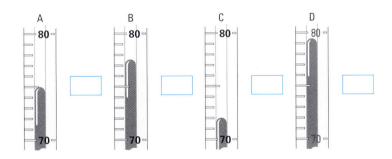

What is the temperature difference between thermometer A and B? °C

Making observations

Not all investigations will need measurements taken. Sometimes you will need to make observations.

When you make observations, you must make **all** observations and not just some of them.

All changes are important, but you may not know why at the time.

When you heat something in a test tube, you might look for:

- a change in colour (make sure you record the colour at the start as well as at the end)
- a change in state e.g. solid ➞ liquid or liquid ➞ gas
- a gas being given off
- a precipitate in the bottom of the test tube
- a noise when a solid decomposes.

As you heat sulphur in a test tube, you can make at least ten observations.

At the start sulphur is a pale yellow solid.

1. Sulphur melts at a low temperature.
2. It forms a pale amber coloured liquid.
3. The liquid is free-flowing at this stage.
4. The liquid then goes darker in colour.
5. It eventually turns black.
6. The liquid is now thick and hard to pour.
7. The liquid starts to boil.
8. The sulphur catches alight.
9. The flame is a pale blue.
10. There is a choking smell.

Notice how detailed the observations are.

Do not just say something is yellow. There are many different colours of yellow.

Use descriptions like amber yellow, canary yellow, banana yellow, dark yellow.

Make a list of six different descriptions of the colour green.

1 _____
2 _____
3 _____
4 _____
5 _____
6 _____

To get good marks for observing as part of skill O you must give detailed observations. Pretend you are explaining what you can see to a friend at the other end of a telephone.

Now we are going to make some measurements.

Look at the diagrams showing four more examples of measuring instruments.

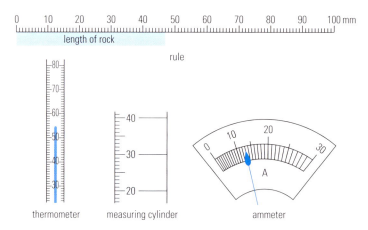

Write down the measurements shown on each piece of apparatus. Don't forget the units.

a rule _____

b thermometer _____

c measuring cylinder _____

d ammeter _____

Why is the ammeter scale more difficult to read than the others?

_____

_____

2 Skill Area O

For a mark of six or above in Skill Area O you have to repeat readings where necessary.

You must ask yourself if it is possible to repeat the reading, **under exactly the same conditions.**

If it is not possible, write this down and move on.

If it is possible, take two or three sets of readings and average them.

Use the average reading when you go on to analyse your results.

A student has mixed different volumes of sodium thiosulphate solution, water and dilute hydrochloric acid. She has timed how long it takes for a cross to disappear.

Here is her table of results.

	volume of sodium thiosulphate in cm³	volume of hydrochloric acid in cm³	volume of water in cm³	total volume	time taken for cross to disappear
(i)	35	5	15	55	25 sec
(ii)	5	5	45	55	1.50 min
(iii)	25	5	25	55	35 sec
(iv)	10	5	40	55	1 min 15 sec
(v)	15	5	30	55	1 min
(vi)	45	5	5	55	20 sec

She has made at least four mistakes in her table. Write them down.

1 _____

2 _____

3 _____

4 _____

If we wrote down a table like this, even with our corrections, we might expect our teacher to give us four marks.

The student has not repeated readings, not all readings have units and timings are confused.

In our investigation, we decided to change the mass.

We need to do the experiment at least five times with a different mass each time.

If we have time, we should try to repeat the experiment and find the average result.

mass of sugar in g	time taken to dissolve in s		
	first reading	second reading	average reading
10	12	16	14
20	34	33	34
30	56	61	59
40	84	86	85
50	135	144	140

We have only read our stopwatch to the nearest second.

When we find averages, we do not bother to work these out any more accurately.

If we do make a measurement to 0.1s, then all of our results, and the average, should be to one decimal place.

For example, if our two times were 34.3 seconds and 33 seconds exactly, then we would write these as 34.3s and 33.0s. The average would be 33.7s not 33.65s.

Look back at page 9. Tick off what you think our table is worth.

It seems to have all that we need for six marks.

3 Skill Area A
Analysing evidence and drawing conclusions

There are some important points you must know before you start analysing your results.

- Analysing involves processing your results. It is not enough to repeat your table of results as a sentence.

- If you want to score more than one or two marks you usually must plot some form of graph.

    The graph should have a title.

    Axes of the graph should be labelled. The labels should have quantity and unit.

    The intervals on the axes should be sensible.

    The graph should be as large as the paper permits BUT be careful if you decide to miss out the origin.

- If you want to score more than four marks your graph should contain a line of best fit.

    When you draw graphs in Maths, the line passes through every point you plot.

    In Science, the points you use are a result of doing an experiment.

    All scientists make experimental errors. These are not the same as mistakes. Experimental errors are how accurately you can read an instrument.

    For example a block of wood may be 36.2987 millimetres long. With a metre rule, the best we can record is 36.0 mm or 36.5 mm.

    Do not expect every point of your graph to lie on the line.

A line of best fit, in Science, does not always mean a straight line.

We should aim to draw the best line we can, through points but not being afraid to miss some out.

- As well as drawing a graph, you should also describe it.

Suppose we had chosen to vary the type of sugar instead of changing the mass of one type.

Our results may have looked like this.

type of sugar	time to dissolve
caster	18 s
icing	12 s
cube	49 s
granulated	20 s

Let us look at the different ways we could use this information.

We could simply write:

> We have found out that caster sugar takes 18 s, icing sugar 12 s, cube sugar 49 s and granulated sugar 20 s to dissolve.

All we have done is to repeat our observations as a conclusion.

At best our teacher might consider this worth one mark.

If we arranged the times in order, we would have done some processing.

> We have found that icing sugar dissolves quickest, followed by caster sugar, then granulated sugar. Cube sugar takes the longest.

Now our teacher might consider this worth two marks.

We could draw a simple bar chart.

We cannot use a line graph because there are four different **types** of sugar. A line graph can only be used when the quantities are linked and there is gradual change, for example in temperature, 0 °C, 10 °C, 20 °C, 30 °C, etc.

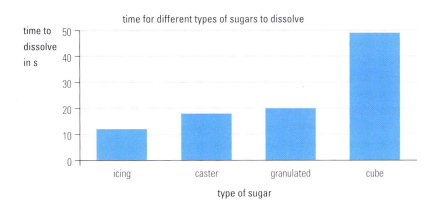

We have processed the results onto a graph and arranged them into order.

We would be on our way to scoring four marks.

Our investigation has mass and time as variables. These are both **continuous variables** so a line graph is the best way to present our results.

Look at the three graphs on pages 28–29. They have been drawn to show our results.

Which graph would you have drawn? _____

Explain why you would draw the graph in this way.

___

___

___

___

Graph 1

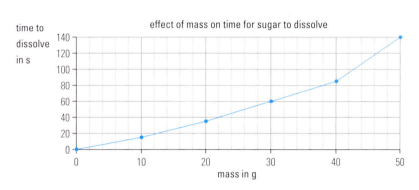

Graph 2

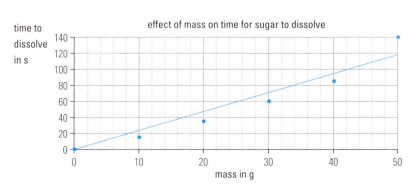

Graph 3

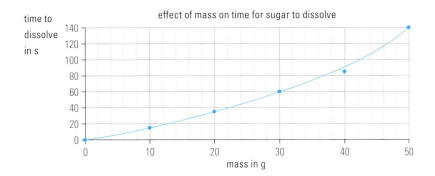

The point (0,0) is called the **origin**. All three graphs pass through the origin. If you think about it, this is right since 0 g of sugar would take 0 s to dissolve.

Graph 1 joins one point to the next with a straight line. This is one of the most common mistakes students make.

As a general rule **NEVER JOIN DOT TO DOT!**

Graph 2 is a very good straight line graph.

Graph 3 is a **line of best fit.**

If you look carefully, there is a trend for the line to get steeper.

Therefore graph 3 is the best one to draw. It is a smooth curve.

The line is closer to all of the points than the straight line.

If you look back to page 10, you will see that we have to write something as well as draw a graph.

If we have drawn a straight line, then we can say that the relationship between mass of sugar and time to dissolve is **linear**.

If a straight line passes through the origin, then we can say that the time to dissolve is **proportional** to the mass. Graphs are only proportional if they are straight AND pass through the origin.

If we have drawn a smooth curve, like graph 3, then we can say a bit more. Perhaps something like:

> As the mass of sugar increases so the time to dissolve increases but at a bigger rate.

This statement coupled with our smooth curve graph, could well deserve five marks.

To get six marks, we have to use our scientific knowledge.

Why does the graph get steeper?

Why does it take more than twice the time to dissolve twice the mass of sugar?

Think about what is happening when things dissolve in water.

If necessary, look up in a textbook about saturated solutions.

Write down why you think the curve is the shape it is.

_____
_____
_____
_____
_____
_____

Now show what you have written to your teacher and ask if it is worth the six marks.

4 Skill Area E
Evaluating evidence

There are some important points you must know before you start evaluating your investigation.

- Most students find Skill Area E is the most difficult skill.
- It is marked out of six not eight like the other Skill Areas.
- There is more to evaluating than writing:

  > I enjoyed doing the investigation and I have learned a lot.

  or

  > The experiment worked well and could not be done better.

- You must look at your results and make comments on them, such as:
  - Did I take enough observations or measurements?
  - Did I check my results by repeating them?
  - Is it possible to repeat the results?
  - Did I get similar results when I repeated them?
  - How close to the line on the graph were my points?
  - Was my method the best one?
- Then make suggestions to improve the experiment you have done.
- Do not start your evaluation by suggesting a different set of variables.

The evaluation of our experiment might include points such as:

When I repeated my readings, they were very similar.

The curve I have drawn on my graph is very close to the points I have plotted.

It took time to pour the sugar into the water.

I started the stopwatch after I had poured it all in, but by then some had started to dissolve.

Write down some more things you could say about the experiment we have been considering.

_____

_____

Here are the results from a different experiment – **'What affects the time for one swing of a pendulum?'**

length of pendulum in cm	time for 10 swings in s	time for 1 swing in s
40	12	1.2
80	18	1.8
120	23	2.3

These results have been plotted on the grid below.

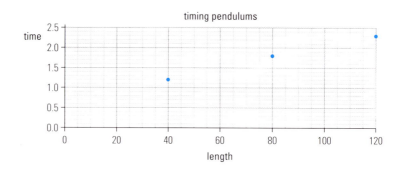

Write an evaluation of this experiment.

_____
_____
_____
_____
_____
_____

What happens to pulse rate during and after exercise?

Whole investigation

You may have carried out an experiment to measure your pulse rate.
You counted the number of beats in 15 seconds and then took some exercise. You then took your pulse rate, for fifteen seconds, each minute for five minutes.

Make a prediction about the effect of exercise on pulse rate.

_____
_____
_____

GCSE Science Foundation Coursework

Use your scientific knowledge to explain your prediction.

_____

_____

You could have the results shown in the table.

time	beats in 15 seconds	heart rate, beats per minute
Before exercise	16	64
Immediately after exercise	24	96
1 minute after exercise	21	84
2 minutes after exercise	18	72
3 minutes after exercise	16	64
4 minutes after exercise	16	64
5 minutes after exercise	16	64

Now, on the grid plot these results and draw a graph.

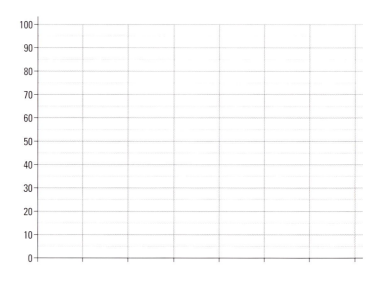

What can you conclude from these results?

___

Use your scientific knowledge to explain your results. Do they support your prediction?

___

Look at the table. Are your results for heart rate in beats per minute more accurate than those for counting the number of beats per 15 seconds? Explain why.

___

Some of the results in the table are easy to repeat and some are not.

Which results are easy to repeat and which are not?

___

How could you attempt to show that the experimental results were good?

_____

_____

_____

By now, you should know a lot more about Sc1 investigations.

You do not know which of your investigations will be used in your assessment.

It is important that you make sure each investigation is done as well as you can.

Record how well you think you are doing and how well your teacher thinks you are doing on pages 9 and 10.

Your final mark

Not all of your marks count towards your final Sc1 mark.

Double Award Science

You have to do at least three pieces of assessed practical work.

Usually you will do far more than this.

Your marks must come from all three subject areas Sc2 (Biology), Sc3 (Chemistry) and Sc4 (Physics).

One mark must also come from a whole investigation.

You must have a mark in each Skill Area.

Single Award Science

You have to do at least two pieces of assessed practical work.

Usually you will do far more than this.

Your marks must come from at least two subject areas Sc2 (Biology), Sc3 (Chemistry) or Sc4 (Physics).

One mark must also come from a whole investigation.

You must have a mark in each Skill Area.

Certificate of Achievement

How marks are awarded depends on the Examination Group.

Ask your teacher to explain to you how you score marks.

External Moderation

At the end of your course, your school sends work to a moderator.

The moderator works for the Examination Group.

The job of a moderator is to make sure that schools across the country, and abroad, have all marked work to the same standard.

This makes sure that you, and all other students, are being treated fairly.

The marks your teacher has given you may be changed, upwards or downwards.

This does not happen very often.

You cannot be 100% certain that the marks your teacher has given will be the marks used to calculate your final grade.

Final words

Good luck!

NOTES

NOTES